UFOs & ETs

A biblical and cultural exploration of aliens

WHY ALL THE INTEREST IN UFOs? • WHAT DOES THE BIBLE SAY? • HOW
DO WE EXPLAIN ALL THOSE UFOs? • IS THERE AN ALIEN INVASION OF A
DIFFERENT TYPE? • HAVE EXTRATERRESTRIALS VISITED EARTH IN THE PAST?

A POCKET GUIDE TO . . .

UFOs & ETs

A biblical and cultural exploration of aliens

Answers
IN GENESIS™

Petersburg, Kentucky, USA

Reprinted May 2016

ISBN: 978-1-62691-328-8

Printed in China.

AnswersInGenesis.org

Table of Contents

Introduction

A 2012 survey reported that more than a third of Americans believe that aliens have visited Earth, whereas only about a sixth of Americans do not think aliens have visited—and nearly half of Americans are undecided. Since those who believe in flying saucers outnumber non-believers by two-to-one, it is obvious that people are fascinated with the possibility of aliens visiting Earth. This belief in aliens permeates our society and is evidenced by many cultural references to UFOs and ETs.

Given this great interest, it is not surprising that at Answers in Genesis we are frequently asked questions about UFOs and ETs. It seems that nearly everyone today is curious about the possibility that extraterrestrials might have visited Earth or are alive somewhere in the universe. There certainly are many resources available that explore various explanations for UFOs. However, there is a shortage of resources that approach this question from a biblical worldview. This Pocket Guide is intended to help fill this need. Christians ought to take the Bible as their ultimate authority in all matters, so we should turn to Scripture on the question of UFOs as well. Since the term UFO is of recent origin, we shouldn't be surprised that the Bible does not directly address UFOs. On the other hand, the Bible does give us information about related matters, so we can use that information to develop a biblical response to UFOs.

For instance, when most people ask about UFOs, they are thinking in terms of flying saucers. So for the sake of argument, let's just suppose that flying saucers exist. What are flying saucers, and where do they come from? Presumably, flying saucers are spaceships piloted by alien astronauts from other planets. The question, then, comes down to whether or not intelligent life exists on other planets.

Many people attempt to answer the question of extraterrestrial life, or ETs, by investigating how many planets might be orbiting other stars, what percentage of those planets might harbor life, and, more importantly, what percentage of planets have intelligent life on them. If intelligent life exists elsewhere, then is it possible that civilizations on other planets may be much more advanced than ours and might have taken the big step of interstellar travel to visit our world? To many people, the answer to that question is an overwhelming "Yes!" But that answer sort of skips over the question of the origin of life. Hidden within that answer is the tacit assumption of evolution—wherever conditions for life are conducive, life inevitably will arise.

Is this the way that a Christian ought to approach the question of life elsewhere? We know that life on Earth did not arise spontaneously. Rather, God created life (Genesis 1), and man has a special status because God created him in His image (Genesis 1:26–2:25; Psalm 8:3–8). Would it be within the character and practice of God to permit life to naturally arise elsewhere in the universe? No. It would seem that if life exists elsewhere, God created that life. Hence, the question of whether life exists elsewhere is theological in nature.

Man's special status leads to two classifications of life on Earth: man and everything else. God made man in His own image and in His likeness, and God has given man dominion over the earth and other living things on the earth (Genesis 1:26–27). Everyone recognizes that people have intelligence that is vastly beyond the intelligence of animals. Man being created in God's image and likeness certainly includes high intelligence, but it encompasses far more. For now, let's just consider man's intelligence as a characteristic of being made in God's image and likeness. If aliens from other planets can travel to Earth, they obviously must possess technology far beyond any that man has made. Therefore, those beings must be very intelligent. As such, are they made in the image and likeness of God as well?

If so, then do those beings have the capacity to have a relationship with our Creator? Do they have eternal souls? Are these beings in need of salvation? And was it because of Adam's transgression or because of the transgression of an "Adam" on each of their planets? In Romans 8, Paul speaks of the taint of Adam's sin affecting all of creation. Did Adam's sin bring corruption on other planets where intelligent life exists? If so, is that just? Did Jesus' atonement on Earth suffice to atone for their sins, or did Jesus have to be born, live, die, and rise again on countless other planets? These tough questions have nothing to do with science, so to the Christian, science doesn't have much to say about these issues. We will explore these questions and more in this Pocket Guide.

As you consider these ideas, keep in mind that UFO stands for "unidentified flying object." Any object visible in the sky that a person cannot identify qualifies as a UFO. But that doesn't automatically mean that a UFO is a flying saucer. There can be many other explanations for UFOs, including natural phenomena. The word "natural" is simply a term that we use to describe the order that God has imposed upon His creation. The Bible tells us that Jesus is the Creator (John 1:1–14) and that this world is sustained by the power of His word (Colossians 1:17; Hebrews 1:3). Many UFOs are explainable in terms of natural phenomena, so in this very real sense, UFOs are well within the normal, God-ordained operation of the world.

Why All the Interest in UFOs?

Star Trek, Star Wars, ET, Close Encounters of the Third Kind, Alien, Men in Black, Dr. Who, The X-Files. It is clear that stories of extra-terrestrials have captured the imagination of Hollywood. But this fascination with aliens is not limited to movies and television—references to visitors from outer space can be found widely in our culture. This goes far beyond popular culture, however, because scientists have taken the possibility of life elsewhere very seriously. For instance, the first SETI (Search for Extra Terrestrial Intelligence) experiment was launched more than a half century ago.

For two decades the Air Force conducted official investigations of UFO sightings. And more recently, scientists have come to recognize an entire discipline called, "astrobiology," to study the possibility of alien life. There is now even a scientific journal, *Astrobiology*, dedicated to this relatively new field. Why is there such great interest in extraterrestrials? There are several reasons for this phenomenon. We will explore some of those reasons in this Pocket Guide. More importantly, we will attempt to answer these questions from a biblical viewpoint, an approach that is glaringly absent among so much discussion of this subject.

Defining the terms

But first, let's define a few terms. What is a UFO? The term *UFO* is short for Unidentified Flying Object. Whenever a person sees an object in the sky that he cannot identify, it is a UFO. However, that does not mean that the UFO is a flying saucer—a space ship piloted by LGMs (Little Green Men) from another world. Rather, it means that the object in question merely is in the sky and is yet unidentified. If, upon further examination, someone can identify the UFO, it becomes an *IFO*, or Identified Flying Object.

Many objects have been reported as UFOs—bright stars or planets, meteors, aircraft, reflections, mirages, and will-o'-the-wisp to name just a few. But just because a UFO remains unidentified, it does not mean that it is evidence of alien visitation. It may simply mean that no one has yet figured out what it was. There are some rare atmospheric but natural phenomena, such as ball lightning, that are not yet understood. While the term UFO is specific and well-defined, a flying saucer is not. At the very least, we must keep in mind that a UFO and a flying saucer are two, very different things.

Identifiable origins

We can trace the fascination with flying saucers and visiting space aliens, at least in the United States, to two events that occurred only a few weeks apart in the summer of 1947. On the afternoon of June 24, 1947, Kenneth Arnold, a civilian aviator, was flying a small plane near Mount Rainier in Washington when he spotted nine, unusual objects flying in the sky. Arnold considered but then eliminated several possible identifications, such as other aircraft and flying geese. He estimated the speed of the objects at nearly 2 ½ times the speed of sound, but later reduced that estimate to a little less than twice the speed of sound. At that time, no aircraft had yet broken the sound barrier, so such a speed would have been remarkable.

Upon landing his plane in Yakima an hour later, Arnold reported to the airport manager what he had seen, and word quickly spread. The next day, a reporter interviewed Arnold, and in telling and retelling what he had seen, Arnold used various terms to describe the shape of the objects that he had seen such as "convex," "half moon," "pie pan," and "disk." He likened their

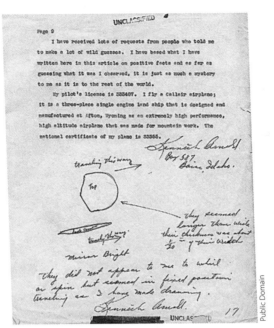

Kenneth Arnold's report

motion in the sky to saucers skipping on water. Although Arnold used the word saucer in describing their motion, he did not actually describe the appearance of what he saw as saucers. Nor did he use the term "flying saucer."

However, news accounts soon morphed his words, coining the new term "flying saucer." Arnold believed what he had seen were not mirages, as the US Air Force eventually ruled. At the time, Arnold considered the possibility that he had seen some secret, superfast aircraft, but the Air Force never acknowledged that it had yet launched any vehicles capable of such speeds in 1947. So, Arnold eventually concluded that what he had seen were craft visiting the earth from another planet. But he was not alone in his conclusion. By the early 1950s, millions of people believed in flying saucers.

In the wake of Arnold's experience, many other people were soon seeing flying saucers, though virtually no one had seen them before 1947. Why was this? Was the earth suddenly being visited by extraterrestrials? If so, why? Perhaps a better explanation could be that now people were looking at things differently. But if so, why was there such a rapid change in the thinking of so many people? The most likely answer to that question is simply that the time was right.

A shifting center

Today we understand that the earth is just one of eight planets orbiting the sun, that the sun is a star, and that there are planets orbiting many other stars. We take these ideas for granted, but this is a very modern view. In ancient times, people thought that the earth, the sun, and the moon were unique. Driving this idea was the geocentric theory, the belief that the earth remained stationary while the sun, moon, and stars orbited the earth. As long as the earth was the center of the universe, it did not make sense to think of life elsewhere in the universe, because any other earth-like place would have to orbit the earth.

Very few people in the ancient world believed the heliocentric theory, that the earth orbits the sun along with the other planets. It was less than four centuries ago that the heliocentric theory replaced the geocentric theory as the dominant view. About that time, astronomers came to realize that the stars were similar to the sun, albeit much farther away. Once people realized that the sun was a star, it was very easy to conceive that just as the sun has orbiting planets, many other stars may have planets orbiting them as well. Only with this paradigm shift was it possible to think of life elsewhere and the possibility that we might visit them or that they might visit us.

While a few people in the ancient and medieval world mused over the possibility of life on other worlds, the first clear exposition of this belief was by Giordano Bruno (1548–1600). Bruno was a Dominican friar, philosopher, and mathematician. He also studied astronomy, which at that point was comingled with astrology. Early in his life, Bruno accepted the heliocentric theory, and he soon embraced the concept that there likely were planets orbiting other stars. From there it was a modest step to suppose that life might exist on many of those other worlds. Unfortunately, the Roman Catholic Church executed Bruno. Since some of Bruno's ideas are so widely accepted today, many people view Bruno as an

Statue of Giordano Bruno

insightful scientist and a martyr of modern science. For instance, the first episode of the 2013 *Cosmos* TV series (which was a revival of the late Carl Sagan's 1981 PBS series by the same name) explicitly made this case.

However, Bruno had absolutely no evidence for his beliefs about life on alien worlds, for he said that many of those beliefs came in dreams. Furthermore, Bruno's belief in life on other worlds had little to do with his execution. Rather, Bruno was found guilty of heresy for denying cardinal doctrines of Christianity, such as the Trinity, the Deity of Jesus Christ, the Virgin Birth, and the Resurrection. While we cannot support the execution of Bruno for his beliefs, we must keep in mind that his ideas about science were not what got him into trouble, so he was not a martyr for science, let alone a good scientist.

A few decades after Bruno's death, nearly everyone abandoned the geocentric theory in favor of the heliocentric theory, and the realization that the stars are similar to the sun, but much farther away, soon followed. This gradually led to belief in the plurality of worlds—that life exists on planets orbiting other stars.

The first aliens

By the early nineteenth century, belief in the plurality of worlds was common. For instance, late in the summer of 1835, *The Sun* newspaper of New York ran a six-part series of articles supposedly about great discoveries of a civilization on the moon that the famous English astronomer Sir John Herschel had made using a large telescope in South Africa. The stories were accompanied by fanciful drawings of flying men living on the moon. Many people were taken in by this science fiction hoax because it fit so well with their beliefs.

Incidentally, this widespread belief in life on other planets was the world into which Joseph Smith (1805–1844), the founder of the Church of Jesus Christ of Latter-day Saints (the Mormon Church), was born. Accordingly, Mormon doctrine teaches that there are many other inhabited worlds. While Mormons do not generally tell those outside their church about these matters, Mormon theology teaches that Elohim, the God of the Bible, was born a man on the planet Kolob (or, alternately, a planet orbiting a star named Kolob). Through his good works, this man was exalted to godhood and was given a section of this galaxy where he organized our solar system to rule over along with his eternal wife. In similar manner, some

Mormons can progress to become gods and be assigned a portion of the universe to rule over as well.

Science fiction

Science fiction as a genre is a modern invention. Of course, it does not always include aliens or space travel, but they are common themes in science fiction. There were a few writings in early modern times that we could describe as science fiction. These include Johannes Kepler's *Somnium* (published in 1634), Jonathan Swifts' *Gulliver's Travels* (1726), Voltaire's *Mircomégas* (1752), and Mary Shelley's *Frankenstein* (1818). Both *Somnium* and *Mircomégas* involve space travel.

However, it was Jules Verne and H.G. Wells, products of the late nineteenth and early twentieth centuries, who truly defined the genre of science fiction. Their novels sometimes included space travel. But the twentieth century saw great expansion of science fiction stories about space travel and aliens. Over three decades,

Jules Verne   H.G. Wells

starting in 1912, Edgar Rice Burroughs published more than ten novels about Mars. The science fiction magazine, *Amazing Stories*, premiered in 1926. A story about Buck Rogers by Philip Francis Nolan appeared in *Amazing Stories* in 1928, followed by a Buck Rogers comic strip the next year. Then Flash Gordon came on the scene in a 1934 comic strip. And in 1938, Superman debuted in a comic book as an alien baby that was transported to earth by a space ship.

A new medium

Meanwhile, the new medium of film also began to explore science fiction themes, including space travel. The first notable science fiction film was the 1902 short, French, silent film *Le Voyage dans la Lune* (*A Trip to the Moon*) largely inspired by Jules Verne's novels *From the Earth to the Moon* and *Around the Moon*. Then in the 1930s, Buck Rogers and Flash Gordon were brought to the silver screen in the form of popular serials complete with space travel and alien beings.

In 1951, the famous movie *The Day the Earth Stood Still* came out. It

A still from *A Trip to the Moon*

Public Domain

An illustration by Henrique Alvim Corrêa from the 1906 edition of *War of the Worlds* depicting a Martian tripod battling the warship *Thunder Child*

Public Domain

Poster and retouched still from *Forbidden Planet*

was a story about a being from another planet who visited earth. This film was followed two years later by *War of the Worlds*, a movie loosely based on the 1898 H.G. Wells novel by the same title involving a Martian invasion of earth. And the unforgettable *Forbidden Planet* and *Invasion of the Body Snatchers* appeared in 1956.

The 1950s saw many other science fiction films about space aliens. In fact, probably more movies about extraterrestrials visiting earth were made in the 1950s than in any other decade. This is no accident, for this time coincided with the widespread increase in interest in extraterrestrials following the 1947 incident near Mount Rainier. Furthermore, the recent development of ballistic missiles made the possibility of space travel a near reality. This time also coincided with the beginning of the Cold War, and many of these movies were metaphors about it. Aliens from outer space made a convenient vehicle for exploring the danger that the godless hordes of Communism presented to the West.

Over the airwaves

Radio was not left out of the fascination over visitors from outer space. On October 30, 1938, Orson Welles coproduced, directed, and starred in CBS radio's *The Mercury Theatre on the*

Orson Welles meets with reporters in an effort to explain that no one connected with the *War of the Worlds* radio broadcast had any idea the show would cause panic

Air live adaptation of H.G. Wells' *War of the Worlds*. The story was told in a series of on-the-scene news reports of invaders from Mars. Although the radio show (and its intermission) were preceded and followed by announcements that it was only a radio play adaptation of the book, the show caused widespread panic across the United States.

Why were so many people swept up with this radio broadcast, thinking that it was a real invasion? One answer may be that it reflected the growing anxiety over the seeds of war in Europe (the beginning of World War II was just ten months away). However, no one would believe that there was a Martian invasion unless they already believed that Martians likely existed. That is, the possibility of a Martian invasion conformed to what people already thought.

Scientific support

This sort of thinking affected scientists as well as laypeople. The astronomer Percival Lowell, a contemporary of Verne and Wells, became convinced that Mars was inhabited. Lowell founded Lowell Observatory in Flagstaff, Arizona primarily to investigate Mars. He used his large telescopes there to map the Martian surface. Lowell saw many wispy, straight lines on Mars that he interpreted

Public Domain

Percival Lowell observing Venus from the Lowell Observatory in 1914

as an extensive canal system on its surface. With no visible bodies of water, Mars obviously was a dry planet. However, there are polar ice caps on Mars that grow and shrink from winter to summer.

At the same time, Lowell thought that he saw subtle seasonal color changes between brown and green, suggesting plant life. Assuming that the ice consisted of water, Lowell reasoned that the Martian civilization constructed the canals to transport precious water from higher latitudes to lower latitudes to grow food and provide for other needs of the civilization. In 1965, Mariner 4 flew past Mars and sent back a few photos showing only about 10% of the Martian surface. The photos were quite shocking because they revealed many craters on Mars' surface, something that few, if any, astronomers expected. This suggested that Mars was much more like the moon than the earth. Later space probes to Mars have extensively mapped the planet's surface and have even landed on the planet.

Atlas Agena D with Mariner 4
just before launch at Cape
Canaveral, November 28, 1964

The extensive mapping of Mars has shown that none of Lowell's canals were real, so what happened? Lowell was pushing his telescopes to their limits, and many people now think that Lowell's brain connected faint features that he saw on Mars' surface with straight lines. In other words, Lowell's canals were an optical illusion. Some people have quipped that Lowell found evidence of intelligence—the question was, "Which end of the telescope was the intelligence on?"

Lowell was not the only person who saw canals on Mars, but most other astronomers did not see them. Apparently, those who saw canals saw them frequently. That is, what Lowell saw was consistent with what he expected to see. This is a common phenomenon among laypeople and scientists. We interpret what we observe in terms of what we already know or think that we know.

This may explain why there was such an explosion of interest in flying saucers in the middle of the twentieth century. By this time, people were so conditioned by popular culture and other factors to believe in life on other planets that it was easy to believe that unexplained phenomena were alien visitations. People who believe in alien life and that the alien life might visit the earth are far more inclined to interpret a UFO in terms of alien visitation than would someone who does not believe in life elsewhere in the universe.

The second incident—Roswell

The other important event in 1947 was a story in the July 8 issue of the *Roswell Daily Record*, a newspaper in Roswell, New Mexico. A front-page headline proclaimed, "RAAF Captures Flying Saucer on Ranch in Roswell Region." The RAAF in the story was the Roswell Army Air Field (later renamed Walker Air Force Base). The newspaper reported that a local rancher had found a disk and other debris on his ranch. The rancher had found the debris a few weeks before, and while he was curious about what it was, he had thought little of it at the time. Only after hearing news reports of the other event of flying disks near Mount Rainier did the rancher begin to think that his find might be significant. The rancher contacted the local sheriff, who in turn contacted officials at RAAF.

As word of the find spread, along with the sensational *Roswell Daily Record* headline, officials at RAAF hastily issued a press release and held a press conference. The press release used the term "flying disk," but only because that was what was being described

in local accounts. In the press release and at the press conference, RAAF officials stated that the debris was from a weather balloon and its attached equipment that had crashed in a severe thunderstorm. Other newspapers around the country carried the story, but at that time everyone was satisfied with the statements from RAAF personnel, so the story quickly faded. The story remained buried for about thirty years. However, other events eventually brought what has become known as the "Roswell Incident" back into the limelight.

Right after Kenneth Arnold saw his flying disks in June, 1947, hundreds of other pilots began reporting similar incidents. In response to this, in 1948 the US Air Force conducted Project Sign, a secret investigation of UFOs. The final report of Project Sign was issued early in 1949, and it officially concluded that there was not enough data to determine the origin of some UFO sightings. However, prior to the final report, the majority of the people conducting the investigation favored an extraterrestrial origin of some UFOs.

Dissatisfied with that conclusion, the Air Force rejected it, a different conclusion was reached, Project Sign was dissolved, and it was replaced by Project Grudge. Project Sign's report was not declassified until years later. Project Grudge was more open, and it issued its report in 1949, but continued to operate with limited capacity until 1951. The Grudge report officially concluded that there was no evidence of extraterrestrial activity. This conclusion was accompanied by a public relations campaign to allay the growing anxiety of the US public over the possibility of extraterrestrial visitations to the earth.

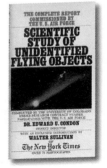

The Air Force conducted Project Blue Book between 1952 and 1970. There was a rash of UFO sightings in 1965, and many people disagreed with the conclusions that the Project Blue Book reached about those sightings. In response to that criticism, the Air Force funded the Condon Committee, under the direction of the physicist Edward Condon at the University of Colorado (1966–1968). Issued in early 1969, the Condon Report found no clear evidence of an extraterrestrial origin for UFOs. The report further recommended that the Air Force cease further formal investigations of UFOs, which led to the end of Project Blue Book shortly after that. This decision, as well as the conclusion of the Condon report, had many critics.

By the end of the 1960s there was such widespread distrust of the various Air Force-sponsored investigations of UFOs that it became a common belief that the sponsored reports were attempts to hide the truth. These suspicions were further fueled by disenchantment with the Vietnam War and the Watergate scandal. By the late 1970s, confidence in the government had fallen to the point that all sorts of various conspiracy theories had gained considerable traction in society, including conspiracies about UFOs.

It was in this environment that several popular authors capitalized upon the Roswell incident of three decades earlier. These authors wrote books, seizing upon supposed inconsistencies in the story. For instance, the RAAF press release initially reported that the rancher had found the debris a few days earlier when in actuality it had been a few weeks earlier. That small detail probably was deemed insignificant at the time. Furthermore, the release used the term "flying disk," though that term was not used again, most likely because this was the term being discussed in the community at that time. This fact was spun into a supposed on-the-spot Air Force officer, in a position of knowledge and authority, opining that he thought that the debris was a space ship before being ordered by his superiors to change his story.

A whole cottage industry of retelling the Roswell incident has grown up since. These revisions also included interviews with many people who claimed to be witnesses to certain things at the time, but these interviews were conducted decades after the events supposedly happened. Included in these were accounts of iconic, dead aliens allegedly recovered at the scene and transported to a freezer (and still kept) at Wright Patterson Air Force Base near Fairborn, Ohio, where Project Blue Book and other investigations were headquartered. Thus, the rather routine incident near Roswell was transformed into a legend.

The real cover-up

However, the conspiracy theorists were right about one thing concerning the incident in Roswell—there was a cover-up. The object that crashed near Roswell in June, 1947, was not a weather balloon at all. Rather, it was a balloon carrying very sensitive microphones to a high altitude in order to detect sound waves from Soviet, atomic bomb tests. This was a top secret US Army Air Force project called Project Mogul to detect and monitor progress of the Soviet Union's atomic bomb program.

Being at the beginning of the Cold War, with tensions running very high, it is understandable that the military did not want word of this project leaking out. Something as sensational as a crashed alien spacecraft was sure to keep the story going and could have led to exposure of Project Mogul. So RAAF issued its press release in an attempt to cover up its involvement in the project. It was not until the 1990s that the Air Force officially declassified Project Mogul and revealed the truth of what happened near Roswell. Of course, to the UFO conspiracy theorists, this was merely the latest twist in the Roswell story and proof of the Air Force's attempt to cover up evidence of alien visitations.

Consequently, there is a tremendous sociology involved with UFOs. People have always encountered strange phenomena that they have difficulty interpreting. We tend to understand things in terms of what we believe, and those beliefs are largely based upon our assumptions. In modern times, people have been conditioned to believe in extraterrestrial life. Hence, it is very easy for some to interpret phenomena in terms of alien spacecraft, especially when an idea has been planted in our minds, as was done by the 1947 incident near Mount Rainier.

In times past, many of these things would have been interpreted differently. Even today, those who are less inclined to believe in extraterrestrials are far more likely to look for explanations other than space aliens when they see peculiar things in the sky. To Christians, it is vital that we develop and employ a biblical worldview rather than one imposed upon us by the world. Let's explore that next.

What Does the Bible Say?

*T*he Bible contains answers to all sorts of questions (2 Timothy 3:14–17; 2 Peter 1:2–4, 1:19–21), so we ought to turn to it to find answers—even about extraterrestrial life. Alas, the Bible does not seem to address that question directly. Keep in mind that for much of history people did not have a worldview that could conceive to even ask about extraterrestrials, so the question of extraterrestrial life is a more modern problem. However, the Bible is not entirely silent on this subject because it does address some fundamental questions of our existence, which, in turn, can shed light on the question of extraterrestrial life.

How did it start?

One such question is the origin of life. How did life on earth arise? In the past, some people have avoided that question by assuming that life on earth has always existed. However, the world would have to be eternal for life to be eternal. But the second law of thermodynamics shows us that energy becomes less useful with time. We define *entropy* to quantify the lack of usefulness of energy in the world. If the universe were eternal, then energy would have had more than enough time to be at maximum entropy now. Life requires the use of energy, so if energy were already at maximum entropy, life would not be possible. Therefore, the world and life cannot be eternal. Since life is not eternal, there are only two possible answers to the question of where life came from—either someone created life, or life arose by natural processes. We call the first possibility creation; the second possibility is evolution.

If life exists on other planets, where did it come from? Again, there are two possible answers to that question—creation or evolution. First, let us consider evolution. If life evolved from non-living things on earth, would we expect life to have arisen on some other planets as well? If life arose spontaneously only on earth and nowhere else, then that would make life on earth unique by definition.

However, if life is unique to earth, then it makes the earth and life on earth special. It is extremely unlikely that the earth is uniquely special by chance alone, so if the earth is special, then that would at least hint of creation. Therefore, most people who believe that life arose on earth by chance believe that life naturally arises wherever the conditions for life are conducive. There are hundreds of billions of stars in our Milky Way galaxy. If it is common for stars in the galaxy to have orbiting planets, and if only a tiny fraction of planets were conducive for life, that still would leave a large number of worlds where life is possible. This is a probability argument. Is there any way to quantify that probability?

What are the odds?

The astronomer Frank Drake did the first SETI (Search for Extra Terrestrial Intelligence) study in 1960. Drake reasoned that if life existed elsewhere in our galaxy, and if life on some planets developed civilization to the point that radio communication were possible, then we ought to be able to eavesdrop on some of that communication. The following year, Drake expressed the probability of finding other technologi-

Photo by Raphael Perrino

Dr. Frank Drake

cally advanced civilizations with his famous equation:

$$N = R \times f_p \times n_e \times f_l \times f_i \times f_c \times L$$

Where:

N = number of civilizations in our galaxy with which communication might be possible

R = average number of stars formed per year in the galaxy

f_p = fraction of stars that have planets

n_e = average number of planets that could support life per star

f_l = fraction of planets that could support life on which life actually develops

f_i = fraction of planets with life that go on to develop intelligent life (civilization)

f_c = fraction of civilizations that develop technology (radio) that we can detect

L = length of time for which such civilizations release detectable radio signals

Many people consider Drake's equation to be good science, but until recently, none of the seven factors in the equation were known—all seven were guesses. The first term, R, cannot be measured, but rather its value typically is a guess based upon one's ideas of how stars might form. The second factor, f_p (the fraction of stars that have planets), was entirely guess work until recent years. In the 1990s, astronomers began detecting extrasolar planets, which are planets that orbit other stars. At the time of this writing (early 2015), there are nearly 2,000 known planets orbiting other stars, but that number is sure to increase. The sample is far from complete, but it appears that planet systems around stars are pretty common, so f_p is probably large. It may be that close to half of all stars have planetary systems. If so, then f_p would be 0.5.

As for the third term, n_e (the average number of planets that could support life), again the sample size is low. However, of the nearly 2,000 known extrasolar planets, none are readily conducive to life. Of the known planets, the only one that is suitable for life is the earth. Therefore, using the data now in hand, we can estimate the value of n_e. If we include solar system planets, n_e is $1/2000 = 0.0005$. However, is it proper to include the solar system (the earth)? We know that life exists here, and the question is whether life exists elsewhere. Therefore, given the nature of the question, it is not proper to include the earth. Furthermore, many experiments require a control, an unchanging situation while other variables may change in other parts of the experiment. In a sense, the earth and solar system serve as a control. If we exclude solar system planets, then n_e is zero.

As for the other four factors, they are a matter of conjecture based upon one's assumptions and degree of optimism. Keep in mind that if even one of the seven factors is zero, the product of Drake's equation will be zero regardless of whatever values the other six factors may have. Therefore, evolutionists have a vested interest in all seven factors being nonzero if they wish to avoid a unique status for the earth. Note, however, that the limited data accumulated thus far indicates that one term, n_e, is zero. From this we can conclude by using the best science now available that life does not exist elsewhere in the universe.

The biblical calculation

How might a person who believes in biblical creation evaluate these seven factors? Those who believe the Bible see purpose in the world around us. For instance, the book of Isaiah states,

> For thus says the Lord, who created the heavens, who is God, who formed the earth and made it, who has established it, who did not create it in vain, who formed it to be inhabited: "I am the Lord, and there is no other" (Isaiah 45:18).

The earth is not the end product of random events because God made the earth the way it is so that it could support life. There is not even a hint in Isaiah 45:18 that God made any other place in the universe with this purpose in mind. Biblically, we can conclude that the only planets that are suitable for life are those on which there actually is life. So, the biblical estimate of the value of n_e (the average number of planets suitable for life) is related to the estimate of f_l (the fraction of planets where life actually exists).

From the creation viewpoint, if life exists on any other planet, then God created that life. The question is, if God created life on other planets, what purpose does that life serve? Why did God create us? The Westminster Catechism answers that question very well—"the chief end of man is to glorify God and to enjoy Him forever." (1 Corinthians 10:31 and Psalm 16:5–11 are just two passages that support this.) We must conclude that life created elsewhere must, at the very least, glorify God.

The mere existence of life on other worlds could suffice to glorify God, so we might not be surprised if God has created life elsewhere. But what about the part that refers to the chief end of man is to enjoy God forever? This speaks of the relationship that we can have with God. The question of extraterrestrial life generally focuses on beings similar to us, so let's focus on that question. In order to travel to the earth, extraterrestrial beings must be intelligent. They must be able to think, to reason, to create, and to have social interaction. All of these attributes touch upon being created in the image and likeness of God (Genesis 1:26–27). If so endowed, extraterrestrials are immortal souls and can commune with God. This brings us to some serious theological questions. Are these extraterrestrial beings sinners? If so, how did their sin nature come about? In the case of man, it was because of Adam's transgression (Romans 5:12; 1 Corinthians 15:2–22). Would extraterrestrials have fallen because of Adam's sin or because of some other event on their worlds? Would Jesus' atonement for sins here on earth (John 3:16; Romans 5:8) have been sufficient to forgive their sins, or would Jesus have died on countless other worlds as well?

These are tough questions, and they are theological and philosophical in nature, not scientific. Let's start with that last question, first. That is, if there is intelligent life on other worlds, did Jesus Christ have to atone for those other races, too? Belief in the plurality of worlds—that intelligent life exists on other planets—can be traced back at least to Anaximander (610–546 BC). However, the later writings of Plato and Aristotle were far more influential, and they taught that the earth, and hence life on earth, was special. Besides, the plurality of worlds does not make sense in the context of the geocentric theory, which was the cosmology that held sway from ancient times through the medieval period. Only with rise of the heliocentric theory in the seventeenth century does the plurality of worlds make sense.

As mentioned in the previous chapter, four hundred years ago, Bruno was one of the first in the more modern era to espouse the plurality of worlds. However, his ideas on the matter hardly could be called scientific. By the seventeenth century, most people had come to accept the heliocentric theory, and most also realized the possibility of the plurality of worlds. For instance, when he was a young man, John Adams recorded in his diary some thoughts on the matter. On April 25, 1756, the future founding father and President of the United States wrote:

> Astronomers tell us, with good Reason, that not only all the Planets and Satellites in our Solar System, but all the unnumbered Worlds that revolve round the fixt Stars are inhabited, as well as this Globe of Earth. If this is the Case all Mankind are no more in comparison of the whole rational Creation of God, than a point to the Orbit of Saturn. Perhaps all these different Ranks of Rational Beings have in a greater or less Degree, committed moral Wickedness. If so,

I ask a Calvinist, whether he will subscribe to this Alternative, "either God almighty must assume the respective shapes of all these different Species, and suffer the Penalties of their Crimes, in their Stead, or else all these Being[s] must be consigned to everlasting Perdition?"[1]

I must clarify what Adams likely meant by "Calvinist." At that time, the Anglican Church was the dominant denomination in the colonies. In Adams' day, liberal elements had infested the Anglican Church. This is evidenced by the reform movement at the time within the Anglican Church, which became the Methodist Church. Those outside the Anglican Church who opposed the liberal ideas of the day were mostly Presbyterians and the less numerous Baptists. As today, the Presbyterians were Calvinists, but the Baptists at the time largely were, too. Adams obviously meant "Calvinist" derisively, and, at the time, it served as a term referring to conservatives among churches in the colonies.

In fairness to John Adams, he later thought his words a bit too strong, for he wrote the next day:

> The reflection that I penned yesterday appears upon the revision to be weak enough. For first, we know not that the inhabitants of other globes have sinned. Nothing can be argued in this manner till it is proved at least probable that all these species of rational beings have revolted from their rightful Sovereign. When I examine the little prospect that lies before me, and find an infinite variety of bodies in one horizon of, perhaps, two miles diameter, how many millions of such prospects there are upon the surface of this earth, how many millions of globes there are within our view, each of which has as many of these prospects upon its own surface as our planet; great and marvelous are thy works![2]

However, notice that Adams did not revise his thinking. He merely acknowledged that he had made some assumptions that could not be substantiated. He noted how little of this world that he could survey at any time and thus concluded how little of the many other worlds that he would never know about. While Adams, here in these two quotes, gives proper respect for God the Father as Creator, he does not give such respect to God the Son. Notice the mocking tone of his first statement when referring to the atoning work of Jesus. One easily can read in Adams' remarks a liberal, perhaps non-Trinitarian view of Jesus. Skeptics today ask the same sort of questions, but they clearly do not believe in any God, which sets them apart from Adams. However, they are the intellectual descendants of the belief system that Adams had.

To be sure, the question that Adams and modern skeptics ask is a good one—one that more Bible-believing Christians ought to ask. If it were for Adam's sin that God holds ETs accountable, then how just is that? To ETs, Adam amounts to an alien. If ETs are held accountable for Adam's sin, one would expect the atoning work of Jesus Christ on earth to atone for ETs' sins. Can you imagine a gospel message that begins, "A long time ago in a galaxy far, far away . . . "? No, this trivializes the gospel. Equally trivial would be the outcome if each alien race had its own equivalent of Adam who sinned and brought each respective race under the penalty of death. That would require that Jesus be born, live, die, and rise again on each of these planets.

While the Bible does not place the earth or man literally at the center of the universe, man clearly is the center of God's attention. Romans 8:18–25 speaks of the bondage of corruption affecting the whole creation. We understand this to be the consequence of sin entering into the world. Furthermore, 2 Peter 3:10–14 speaks of future redemption of the creation that now exists by its destruction and then the creation of a new heaven and a new earth. How is it, then, that man's sin has affected the entire creation in this way, if there are beings on other planets endowed with the same properties that we have? If Adam's sin has affected the entire creation, then it would seem that extraterrestrials suffer the effects of man's sin though they played no part in the Fall.

Psalm 115:16 states, "The heaven, even the heavens, are the Lord's; but the earth He has given to the children of men." If other races of man-like creatures exist elsewhere, then this verse presents a problem. God has given the earth to man, but the heaven, even the heavens, God reserves for Himself. The phrase, "the heaven, even the heavens" would seem to refer to the totality of existence beyond the earth. That would include any planet upon which other beings exist. That means any man-like creatures that exist elsewhere do not have dominion over their respective planets. Nor could God make the same sort of declaration to these other races as He did to man in Psalm 115:16 without violating the spirit and letter of His statement in this psalm.

We can glean a few more principles from the Bible. Jesus told His disciples that He would leave to prepare a place for them (John 14:2–3). John recorded that when Jesus said this, His disciples did not understand what He meant, but we now know that Jesus was going to heaven. Furthermore, we know that Jesus is now seated at the right hand of the Father (Mark 16:19; Acts 2:33; Hebrews 10:12). Jesus' place with the Father in heaven would seem to preclude multiple missions of redemption on other worlds. Finally, Hebrews 10:12 states that Jesus made one sacrifice for sin forever, which clearly rules out Jesus repeating His role in the plan of salvation throughout the cosmos.

With these considerations, we can infer from Scripture that God did not make beings like us, created in His image and likeness, on other planets. Hence, there are no extraterrestrial beings similar to us to pilot spacecraft to earth. That does not preclude the possibility of so-called simple life, such as bacteria or even plants on other planets. However, considering the character of God and the purposes of plants, such as providing food for man and beast (Genesis 1:29–30), even plant life elsewhere is unlikely. Furthermore, while modern biology considers plants to be alive, the Bible never treats plants as living things. This verse from Isaiah gives a typical treatment of plants: "The grass withers, the flower fades, but the word of our God stands forever" (Isaiah 40:8).

Plants are not said to die, rather they wither and fade. We can make the case that in a biblical sense, plants are not alive anyway. Other organisms, such as bacteria, are even less alive than plants in this sense. Therefore, from a biblical worldview, while plants and bacteria are not the sort of things that we might expect to exist on other planets, their presence on other planets might not compromise a biblical worldview. While the evolution model generally demands that life exists elsewhere, the expectation of the creation model is that life probably is unique to the earth, but intelligent life is definitely unique to earth. Therefore, the terms n_e, f_l, f_i, and f_c in the Drake equation likely are zero. And as previously stated, if any of the seven terms in the Drake equation is zero, then we are alone in the universe.

However, the conclusion from Scripture that we are alone in the universe does not stand alone. Recall that from the best data now available we can conclude that life as we know it is unique to the earth. Hence, at this time, both the Bible and good science agree on this. Evolutionists persist in their belief in life elsewhere in spite of, not because of, the best evidence now available.

The spiritual realm

We must be very clear, however, that this discussion thus far does not include angelic beings. Entire books have been written on angels, though the Bible tells us relatively little about angels. We know that they operate in the world and that they are innumerable (Hebrews 12:22). We know that they operate in the heavens as well (Revelation 12:7). Satan, the prince of the power of the air (Ephesians 2:2), is a fallen angel who rebelled against

God and took one third of the angels with him in his rebellion (Revelation 12:4, 12:9).

Thus we know from Scripture that there are at least two other kinds of beings beyond what we normally encounter on earth: angels and Satan and his followers (often called demons). Since these beings are real and operate on earth and in the heavens, it is possible that some UFOs could be related to the activities of angels or demons. Note that this is not necessarily the case, but it is at least a possibility—a possibility that some Christians seriously consider. We shall explore this further later.

1. Adams, John, and Charles Francis Adams. 1850. *The works of John Adams, second President of the United States.* Boston: Little, Brown and Co. http://books.google.com/books?id=7kt3AAAAMAAJ.

2. Ibid.

How Do We Explain All Those UFOs?

If God did not create life elsewhere in the universe, then how do we explain all of those UFO sightings? There are many possibilities. The immediate goal of any UFO sighting is to convert it to an IFO—moving from "unidentified" to "identified." A person who is not inclined to believe in alien visitations is likely to keep investigating any UFO sighting in search of alternatives to it being a flying saucer. On the other hand, a person who strongly believes in alien visitations is far less likely to investigate a UFO with such a skeptical eye. This reinforces the concept that people tend to see in things what they expect to see—a person is far more likely to see flying saucers if they expect to see them, while those who do not believe in flying saucers are far less likely to see them. In times past, when belief in extraterrestrial aliens was not common, people did not interpret unusual phenomena in the sky in terms of flying saucers. There are many everyday objects that can masquerade as unusual, so let's discuss a few of these.

Unfamiliar flying objects

Since few people are familiar with the night sky, a bright star or a bright planet can attract the attention of most people. If for instance, a person is traveling in a vehicle, the apparent shift of foreground objects like trees, hills, or buildings with respect to the star or planet can give the mistaken impression that the star or planet is moving with respect to the ground. But in reality, it is the motion of the vehicle that is causing the apparent motion of the relatively stationary object in the sky.

Aircraft in the sky are common today, but how many people really study the motion and appearance of aircraft? Sometimes a plane can fly or display lights in a manner that is different from how many people expect them to appear. This, too, can look odd to many casual observers, leading them to think that they have seen a spacecraft. Something of this nature happened to me when I was in high school. Riding along in a car one day, I happened to look up, and I saw a silver object in the sky. At the time it appeared to be the edge-on view of a silver disk in the air. My father, the driver of the automobile, noticed that I was intently looking at something, so he asked what it was. When I pointed it out to my father, he, too, had no idea what it was. Eventually, the object slowly turned from being edge-on. It turned out to be an Air Force plane (I grew up near Wright Patterson Air Force Base). What I had seen was the fuselage and fuel tanks on the ends of the wings that appeared to merge into a single object (I believe that it may have been a T-33). Up to that point, it certainly looked like a flying saucer. However, my father and I applied tools of investigation (we kept watching) so that we were able to convert the UFO to an IFO. If the plane had disappeared into a cloud, we might not have ever figured out what it was, but that would not have made it a flying saucer.

There also are many unusual-appearing experimental aircraft. Many test flights are conducted at night, which makes identification more challenging. Even if one sees a daytime test flight, the appearance of experimental planes and other flying craft can be so odd as to prevent some people from correctly identifying them as aircraft. Some experimental aircraft are secret projects under development by the military. Since these planes do not "officially" exist in public knowledge, it is not possible to identify exactly what they are.

Some UFO sightings have been correlated with weather balloons. Weather balloons are launched twice daily from more than

800 locations around the world. That is more than a half million weather balloon launches per year. And that does not include special weather balloon launches in addition to the normal twice daily, nor does it include the many other balloons launched for various scientific investigations other than weather. These balloons are often highly reflective and can be seen for miles. They remain aloft for a long time, and winds carry the balloons considerable distances, so their motion can be obvious. There is a long relationship between UFOs and balloons because the 1947 Roswell incident involved the recovery of debris from a balloon crash site.

Rawinsonde weather balloon just after launch

Public Domain

Some UFO sightings could actually be satellites. There are thousands of artificial satellites that orbit the earth. Many of these are visible to the naked eye as star-like objects moving across the night sky. Satellites move much more slowly than meteors—about as fast as some aircraft move. We see them not because of on-board lights but because they reflect sunlight. Satellites are visible mostly during the summer shortly after dark and before dawn. In the middle of the night and during winter months, the earth's shadow prevents us from seeing them. The behavior of satellites is distinct from aircraft. For instance, unlike aircraft, there are no flashing lights or engine sounds. And in the evening, satellites can disappear as they enter the earth's shadow,

An Iridium flare (middle of sky) and Comet Holmes (blur near branches)

while in the morning they can suddenly appear as they emerge from the earth's shadow.

Larger satellites, such as the International Space Station or space shuttles (when they were still flying) appear very bright, much brighter than aircraft or stars. This, too, appears unusual to many people and can thus qualify as a UFO in their minds. Occasionally a satellite's brightness can "flare." I once experienced a flare while watching a space shuttle pass. A flare is caused by the orientation of flat surfaces, such as solar panels or the wings of the space shuttles, that can reflect light only briefly at a location on the earth's surface. Most notable are the 66 satellites that comprise the Iridium Communications network, used for worldwide phone service and data transmission. An Iridium flare lasts for only a few seconds—as if a bright star suddenly appears where there was none, moves a short distance across the sky, and then disappears. A person not aware of this phenomenon would see this as unusual and could view it as a UFO.

Natural causes

Other than bright stars and planets, there are other natural phenomena in the sky that people have interpreted as flying saucers. Meteors create bright, fast streaks of light in the sky, easily seen at night, though a few very bright ones can be visible in the day. Because meteors resemble rapidly moving stars in the sky, they are sometimes called "shooting stars" or "falling stars." Meteors are small bits of rock or ice from asteroids or comets that burn up as they encounter the earth's atmosphere at an altitude of about 60 miles. As an astronomer, I am amazed at how many people I meet who have never seen a meteor. Meteors really are not that rare—in a dark, clear location it's possible to see a minimum of five to six of them per hour. So when I encounter someone who has never seen a meteor, I am sure that they are not familiar with the night sky at all. And because people tend to be so unfamiliar with phenomena in the sky, it is easy to understand why they would interpret things they see in the sky, such as meteors, in terms of flying saucers.

Aurorae, also known as northern lights (*aurora borealis*) in the northern hemisphere and southern lights (*aurora australis*) in the southern hemisphere, have been known since ancient times. The cause of aurorae is fast-moving, charged particles rushing outward from the sun—the solar wind. As solar wind particles approach the earth, the earth's magnetic field diverts the path of many of these particles. This diversion brings the paths of the particles close to the magnetic poles of the earth where the particles collide with air molecules about 60 miles up. The collisions ionize atoms, and as the electrons recombine with atoms, they emit visible light. The most common color of the light is white, but red and green are often visible, too. Aurorae can be faint broad glows, or the light can emit in spots or in arcs. As the interaction between the solar wind and the earth's magnetic field progresses, the spots and arcs can rapidly move across the sky.

Aurora borealis, or northern lights

© Thinkstock.com

While aurorae are common at high latitudes closer to the poles, they are rare in more temperate latitudes closer to the equator. However, at times when solar flares are common (e.g., near sunspot maximum of the eleven-year sunspot cycle), after a solar flare a gust in the solar wind may approach the earth a day or two later. The increased volume of charged particles forces aurorae farther from the magnetic poles into regions where aurorae are rare. The unusual phenomenon of bright, colorful, moving aurorae has been reported as UFOs.

Cirrus clouds are thin, wispy high altitude clouds made of flat, hexagonal ice crystals. When sunlight passes through these clouds, the light interacts with the ice crystals bending the direction of the light to produce all sorts of interesting halo phenomena. The most common visible halos are called sun dogs. Sun dogs typically appear as two subtly colored patches of light to the left and right of the sun. They appear when the sun is low in the sky with a streak of cirrus clouds obstructing it. These spots, or sun dogs, are

Dramatic sundogs photographed in Fargo, North Dakota, February 18, 2009

at the same altitude as the sun, but are 22° from the sun. Sun dogs are the brightest portions of an entire halo around the sun, which is usually visible when the sun is much higher in the sky. Sun dogs can be seen almost anywhere in the world at any time of the year, but when the sun is high in the sky, they are not nearly as bright as when the sun is lower, near the horizon.

There are other, more subtle halo effects. When the sun is rising or setting, the ice crystals in the clouds can produce a pillar of light centered on the sun. While the conditions to produce a halo around the sun are not that rare, much less common conditions can result in various other arcs in addition to the halo. A full or nearly full moon is bright enough to produce similar phenomena at night. As I mentioned before, people who are not familiar with these phenomena often report them as UFOs.

The appearance of relatively bright clouds in a dark sky can also be interpreted as a UFO. Noctilucent clouds are the highest clouds in the earth's atmosphere (more than 50 miles high). They

Photo by Kevin Cho (Kee Pil Cho)

Noctilucent clouds over Stockholm, Sweden, July 12, 2014

occur at relatively high latitudes. And since they are up so high, they can be illuminated by the sun's rays long after sunset in deep twilight and can be mistaken as UFOs.

Down to earth

One natural phenomenon mistaken for flying saucers is fata morgana, a rare type of mirage. A typical mirage occurs on warm, sunny days when sunlight heats the ground, which, in turn, heats a layer of air in contact with the ground. The speed of light in the warmer air next to the ground is greater than the speed of light in the cooler air above. Grazing incident light coming from above and passing toward the ground through cooler air cannot transmit into the warmer air at the surface where the speed of light is greater. Hence, the light is reflected off of the warmer layer of air. Because the light coming from above usually comes from the sky, a person observing this reflected light normally sees an image of the sky. This gives the illusion that the sky is reflecting a pool of water.

An example of fata morgana where a ship appears
to be floating above the horizon

Photo by Timpaananen

The much rarer fata morgana is caused by a temperature inversion where warmer air lies atop cooler air. Here, the mirage is inverted—light rises at grazing incidence through the cooler air and is reflected off the warmer air above. The light comes not from the sky but from an object on the surface. This object can be almost anything—a distant ship, structure, shoreline, hill, or mountain, to name just some examples. Often, the object is beyond the horizon, below the curvature of the earth, but the reflected light of the fata morgana is visible even if light directly from the distant object is not.

The Air Force concluded that the nine objects that Kenneth Arnold saw were a fata morgana. Since radar uses electromagnetic radiation, a fata morgana can appear on radar even if no fata morgana is visible to the eye. Many ghost objects detected by radar that were reported by radar operators as UFOs apparently were the result of fata morganas. During a UFO investigation, investigators enquire about the weather information at the time of the reported incident. From weather data, it is reasonably straightforward to determine if a temperature inversion occurred and whether or not a fata morgana was possible.

A will-o'-the-wisp is an eerie light usually seen over bogs, swamps, or marshes at night. These lights have been known for thousands of years all over the globe and consequently, go by many names. The most common name in the United States is "swamp gas." One would think that after knowing about it for so long, we would know the exact mechanism responsible for will-o'-the-wisp. But alas, there is no agreement on its cause. Perhaps that adds to its mystique. While will-o'-the-wisp normally occurs at low elevation, people are notoriously poor at estimating the distances of some objects above them. For instance, many people perceive that meteors are up a few hundred feet high at most, when in reality meteors are about 60 miles up.

One gauge that our minds use to estimate distances is to compare how large something appears to how large we think it is. If we think that something is very large yet appears very small, then we conclude that object must be very far away. A will-o'-the-wisp is not very large, but if a person erroneously assumes that it is large, then that person will conclude that the will-o'-the-wisp is far away.

Ball lightning, photographed in Maastricht, the Netherlands, June 2011

Photo by Joe Thomissen

Therefore, a person may perceive that a will-o'-the-wisp is much higher in the sky than it really is. A will-o'-the-wisp often moves, so its motion would be interpreted as flying motion high in the sky when it is actually small and close to the ground. There are cases of UFOs actually being will-o'-the-wisp.

Will-o'-the-wisp is not the only unusual lighting in the sky. For example, ball lightning is a rare phenomenon known since ancient times. However, as recently as a half century ago, few scientists were convinced that it was real. Now it is well recognized, though its origin remains a mystery with about a dozen currently held theories. There are also some unusual forms of electrical phenomena associated with thunderstorms. St. Elmo's fire has been noted since ancient times. It is a coronal discharge from pointed objects, such as masts of sailing ships. And sprites are a form of lightning that extend high above thunderstorms and appear red.

Earthquake lights, resembling aurorae, have been reported before or after earthquakes or other seismic activity. There are several theories to explain earthquake lights, including the piezo-electric effect. Then there are recurring reports of strange lights often seen at one geographical location. A good example of this is the Brown Mountain lights. Brown Mountain is in the Blue Ridge Mountains in western North Carolina. As early as the nineteenth century (though Cherokee Indian legends may go back much further), people have reported strange lights at night over Brown Mountain. Scientists have investigated the Brown Mountain lights and reports of other strange, local lights confined to certain locations around the world, but the causes of these lights remain unknown.

All of these strange lights, from will-o'-the-wisp to the Brown Mountain lights, have been reported as UFOs over the years. Since the causes of some of these phenomena are not really known, in some respect these things remain UFOs (and not IFOs). However, that does not mean that they are flying saucers. Prior to 1947, virtually no one attributed them to extraterrestrial spacecraft. We must continue to investigate these phenomena with a skeptical approach. In time, we will likely develop a plausible explanation consistent with how God created our world to function. But until we can do that, some people will choose to interpret unexplained phenomena in terms of alien visitation because it conforms to their worldview in which they expect such things. However, some of us will continue to search for alternate explanations because our worldview is different.

Just for show

There are other UFO sightings and supposed evidence for extraterrestrial visitors that have actually been hoaxes. For instance, in June, 1947, around the time that Kenneth Arnold reported flying objects near Mount Rainier, two men reported falling debris from a UFO over Maury Island in nearby Puget Sound. One of the men claimed that he later was approached by a man

in a dark suit who told him not to talk about the Maury Island incident. This appears to be the origin of the "men in black" in popular culture surrounding UFO sightings, which also inspired the title of the 1997 movie. The debris turned out to be slag from a local smelter, and one of the men later admitted that the entire thing was a hoax.

Many supposed photographs of flying saucers made over the years turned out to be photos of automobile hubcaps

and other similarly shaped objects tossed into the air. There are many examples of faked lights in the sky. On five nights in January and February in 2009, red lights were seen flying over Morristown, New Jersey. These sightings were reported to the police, which in turn, attracted news coverage. The sightings also received a lot of coverage from people in the UFO industry who are thoroughly convinced that extraterrestrial aliens regularly visit earth.

A couple months later on April 1 (April Fool's Day), Joe Rudy and Chris Russo came forward with video evidence that they had staged the events by attaching flares to helium balloons. Subsequently, authorities charged and convicted Rudy and Russo of disorderly conduct. One must wonder why the UFO hucksters who promoted and capitalized on these events were not charged with some crime.

Similarly, and not too far away, in the early 1980s a rash of unexplained colored lights began to appear at night over the Hudson River Valley. After gaining much attention, it eventually turned out that a small group of pilots flying ultralight aircraft with various, synchronized, flashing, colored lights were responsible. However, even though many people came to expect these lights, reported sightings (probably of the lights of aircraft not on hoax missions) continued even after the Hudson Valley mystery had been solved.

Bringing down the sheaves

In the late 1970s, crop circles began appearing in southern England. Crop circles are circular patterns of flattened plants in fields of grain. Almost immediately, crop circles were interpreted as places where flying saucers either hovered or landed. The appearance of crop circles gradually spread across England and then around the world. With time, some crop circles became very elaborate, with many circles joined into larger patterns. UFO enthusiasts traveled extensively to study various crop circles. They even coined the new term "cereology" as the systematic study of

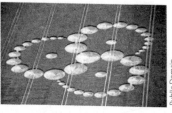

crop circles. The fact that crop circles were almost always in prominent places—along roads and near population centers with no fences—didn't seem to bother cereologists (self-professed experts who studied cereology).

Finally, in 1991 Doug Bower and Dave Chorley formed a crop circle using simple tools made of a plank of wood, rope, and wire in front of a group of journalists. Cereologist Pat Delgado was brought in to examine the crop circle, and he certified the circle as genuine, stating that it could not be manmade. Bower and Chorley said that they had been making crop circles across England since 1978. However, Bower and Chorley were not responsible for all of the crop circles between 1978 and 1991 because other hoaxers had figured out how to make similar circles and joined in on the fun.

Crop circles make an excellent study in the phenomena of UFOs. Crop circles were unknown before 1978. Almost immediately they were interpreted as being produced by flying saucers. Soon, crop circles began to appear almost everywhere. UFO enthusiasts seized upon crop circles as evidence of extraterrestrial visitations. A huge following developed as self-professed experts went on the talk show circuit, appearing on TV and radio programs and even writing books on the subject of crop circles.

To this day, many people continue to believe that crop circles prove that extraterrestrials have visited the earth many times, even though all of it has been thoroughly debunked. What happened? People were prepared to believe in extraterrestrial visitations, and so crop circles conformed to that belief and reinforced it. Once a belief becomes thoroughly ingrained in the minds of most people, it becomes very difficult to dislodge that thinking. Hence, even after crop circles were demystified, some people continued to believe that crop circles were evidence of alien visitations.

How could they think this? It may be that while true believers of ETs acknowledge that many crop circles are fakes, they insist that there remain a few crop circles that are genuine. This is true of all UFO phenomena—the vast majority can be explained, either in terms of converting UFOs to IFOs, or in terms of hoaxes. However, there still remains a very tiny percentage of UFO sightings that yet defy explanation. Do these relatively few sightings constitute evidence of alien visitation? No! Remember, just because we have not yet explained a particular phenomenon as being a natural or manmade thing, it does not mean that they could not be explained in these ways. However, some Christians have developed an interesting theory for yet-unexplained UFOs. That is the subject of the next chapter.

Is There an Alien Invasion of a Different Type?

We have seen that the vast majority of UFO sightings can be explained as various misidentifications of known phenomena. Furthermore, there is a sort of herd mentality in interpreting various objects in the sky. Reports of flying saucers were unknown until after reports of the Mt. Rainier incident in 1947. Then right away, hundreds of other sightings occurred. This sort of thing happens frequently. For instance, after the movie *Jaws* became a sensation in the summer of 1975, there were reports of sharks in waters all over the place. In fact, these locations included freshwater streams and lakes far from the ocean where there could not have been any large sharks. Of course, most of the people making shark reports saw fish or some other objects in the water, but recent events caused them to enlarge and misinterpret what they saw.

In a similar manner, when people hear reports of flying saucers, they tend to interpret anything in the sky that they deem unusual as alien spacecraft. Still, there remains a small portion of reported UFOs that are difficult to explain in terms of things that we understand or at least can document. Does that mean that these sightings are genuine alien visitations? Hardly. It may be that we simply have not yet figured out what these sightings were.

Alleged alien abductions

However, some people have claimed personal experiences that go far beyond merely seeing things in the sky. These people say that they have been abducted by aliens. The supposed purposes of these abductions vary, but allegedly many involve vivisections and other physical examinations of humans. A vivisection is an invasive procedure of surgically opening the body of a living organism for the purpose of observing functioning organs (this is in contrast to dissection, the surgical examination of a dead organism). People making these claims rarely, if ever, offer any physical evidence, such as scars left by the more invasive examinations. That is often explained away by noting that with the advanced technologies that the aliens obviously possess (such as interstellar spacecraft), their medical procedures are similarly advanced so that no scars are left. These claims are very extraordinary to say the least.

While we cannot fully judge the honesty or sincerity of people with such claims, we must question whether these people actually experienced what they claimed. In at least some cases, it is likely that people fabricated their experiences. In other cases, some may be persuaded of the reality of their claimed experiences and, in that sense, are telling the truth as they perceive it. But is it possible that these people may have experienced dreams or may have suffered some delusions? For instance, such accounts are often similar to depictions in movies, so scenes from movies could inspire dreams or delusions that seem very real to those who experience them. In response to these extraordinary claims and the few UFO sightings that are difficult to explain, some Christians have developed an interesting, though controversial, response.

Setting the stage

Some Christians have a view of certain prophetic passages in the Bible that in the end times the Lord will rapture the Church out of this world, either at the beginning, the end, or sometime during a seven-year Tribulation period.[1] The sudden disappearance of millions of people worldwide would be mysterious and naturally would be very troubling to those left behind. In this view, the world will be ruled during the Tribulation by a single leader, the Antichrist. This charismatic leader at first seemingly will have answers to all the world's problems, such as a good response to economic crises and settling wars and other conflicts. Given this, the Antichrist must have a good answer to the question of what happened to all those raptured Christians. What if the Antichrist were to claim that aliens abducted Christians around the world?

This sounds like a very far-out explanation, so how could this sort of answer be sold to the public? If such an answer were abruptly foisted upon the public, it probably would be met with tremendous skepticism. However, according to this theory, if the world had been conditioned into believing in extraterrestrials and the possibility that aliens have been visiting Earth for some time, it would be much easier to convince people that Christians had been removed by alien abduction rather than the rapture. Supporters of this theory point to 2 Thessalonians 2:1–12 as speaking of end times and the rise of the Antichrist. This passage states that God will send a strong delusion so that people will believe a lie rather than the truth. Hence, the combination of preconditioning and the strong delusion would be sufficient to convince most people that alien abductions were responsible for the disappearance of the Church. It would not be necessary that all people be fooled by this, but only that this be the official explanation and that most people believe it. There could be some people, such as those individuals in positions of authority, who may not believe this explanation. All that is required is that they not voice any public opposition to the established explanation.

How could the preconditioning to accept this explanation occur? Those who support this theory generally propose demonic activity underlying UFO phenomena in the world today. This demonic activity could take two forms. One form merely would be to stir up the hearts and minds of many people so that they misinterpret natural and manmade phenomena in the sky in terms of flying saucers. This form of demonic activity also would include influencing self-appointed experts on the subject of alien visitations who supposedly write and speak on the subject with some authority. This form of demonic activity is suggestive in that it involves only influencing thoughts.

The second form of this proposed demonic influence would be far more active. For instance, some unexplained UFOs could be activities of demons designed to appear as flying saucers. Furthermore, some have suggested that demons disguised as space aliens are responsible for reports of abductions and physical examinations. That is, flying saucers and their alien occupants are very real; it's just that Earth has not been invaded by extraterrestrials but instead by fallen angelic beings. According to this theory, it is demonic beings that are carrying out the gruesome experiments on people.

This belief is not universally accepted by Christians, nor should it be. The explanation fits nicely in a particular system of theology and eschatology. However, not all Christians agree with this understanding of end times, the Antichrist, a rapture, and a Tribulation upon which this idea is based. If someone's eschatology is different from this, then the appeal to demonic activity to explain some UFO phenomena and alleged related events is not necessary. Besides, not everyone is convinced of the veracity of those claiming these extraordinary experiences or that there are a significant number of UFO sightings that remain unexplained. Therefore, while this is an interesting explanation, one ought not be dogmatic about it or disrespectful of fellow Christians who disagree with it.

Another satanic possibility

However, there is a biblical basis for the possibility that demons can manifest themselves in appealing terms. In discussing false teachers, the Apostle Paul said that even Satan can transform into an angel of light (2 Corinthians 11:14). Many people who claim encounters with space aliens are seeking, even longing for this interaction. To these people, observing an alien visitation would be a very positive experience. Hence, if some UFO and claimed ET encounters have a demonic origin, then they would qualify as angels of light in the minds of the people involved.

Late in AD 610, Mohammed claimed that he received the first of several revelations. The revelations continued until Mohammed's death 23 years later. These revelations allegedly formed the Qur'an. According to Mohammed's testimony, the revelations were revealed by the angel Gabriel. However, Mohammed said that he did not know who the messenger was and that his first inclination was that the messenger was a devil. He should have trusted his first instinct.

What are the possibilities? Either Mohammed made up the entire story, or he thought that he was telling the truth. If he lied, then Islam is false. If Mohammed thought that he was telling the truth, his story either is true, or he was deceived. Islam and Christianity are incompatible, so if Christianity is true, then Islam is

Public Domain

Mohammed receiving his first revelation from the angel Gabriel. Miniature illustration on vellum from the book often referred to as *The Universal History* or *History of the World* by Rashid al-Din, published in Tabriz, Persia, AD 1307

false. Therefore, either Mohammed lied about his experiences, or Mohammed was deceived. If Mohammed was deceived, then who was the deceiver?

As we shall see in the next chapter, some people have suggested that the being that gave Mohammed his revelations was an ET. That is, they believe that space aliens visited Mohammed. However, a demonic being, perhaps Satan himself, could have been at work. Remember, Satan can appear as an angel of light, and Mohammed soon came to accept that his visitor was Gabriel, who would qualify as an angel of light. The Bible calls Satan a deceiver (2 Corinthians 11:3; Revelation 12:9, 20:3) and the liar and father of lies (John 8:44). Certainly, it would have been within Satan's character to deceive Mohammed.

Joseph Smith claimed that on the night of September 21, 1823, the angel Moroni appeared to him and revealed the existence of buried, golden plates that eventually would become the Book of Mormon. This angel, Moroni, allegedly appeared to Smith on several other occasions over the next few years and supposedly to other early Mormon leaders as well. As with Islam, Mormonism is incompatible with Christianity, so we can ask the same sort of questions about Joseph Smith that we asked about Mohammed. Did Smith and his followers make up these visitations, or did they

Public Domain

The angel Moroni delivering to Joseph Smith the golden plates containing the Book of Mormon

really believe that these visitations were true? If they lied, then Mormonism clearly is false. However, if they thought that they were telling the truth, then either their testimonies are true or they were deceived. If Christianity is true, then Mormonism is false, and Smith and his close group of followers were deceived. If they were deceived, then who was the deceiver? A demonic deception seems a likely explanation, assuming that Smith did not simply lie about these things.

However, as with Mohammed, many people today find it quite plausible that ETs provided the revelations to Smith. Why? For one thing, belief in ETs continues to grow. However, there is another factor. Today there is a widespread belief in universalism, which is the belief that there is some truth in all religions. This is partly driven by a desire not to be judgmental; if we deem a religion to be false, then that seems harsh to many people, particularly when we conclude that followers of that particular religion are deceived. In the post-modern world, it is fashionable to think that there is some truth in everything. With this mindset, it is preferable to think that there are no false prophets among the world's major religions. How then, does one explain the differences between religions? It is not palatable to simply claim that most, and perhaps all, prophets were liars. Rather, it is easier to think that each one in his own way thought that he was doing right and giving honest testimony to what he thought he had experienced.

Within this worldview, satanic deception is not an option. Therefore, what remains? As crazy as it may sound, millions of people now think that alien visitations make much more sense than satanic influences in explaining prophets of the past. The words of Romans 1were never more applicable than to this:

> Although they knew God, they did not glorify Him as God, nor were thankful, but became futile in their thoughts, and their foolish hearts were darkened (Romans 1:21).

This shows that the UFO phenomenon has a spiritual component, as do so many other things today. The postmodern idea of universal salvation is nothing less than an attack on the authority of the Bible. As we shall see in the next chapter, belief that the miracles and the prophets recorded in the Bible are the result of alien visitations has grown to be quite popular. This belief is not possible unless a significant portion of the population readily accepts that flying saucers and ETs are real. Hence it is likely that demonic intervention, at least by suggestion if not by overt action, is involved in the rising interest in UFOs in recent decades. Thus, UFOs represent a new front in the spiritual battle that is in the world around us (Ephesians 6:12).

---

1. As a nondenominational ministry, Answers in Genesis does not take a position on various views of eschatology, assuming those views are drawn out of Scripture. Our statement on eschatology reads: "Jesus Christ rose bodily from the dead, ascended to heaven, and is currently seated at the right hand of God the Father, and shall return in person to this earth as Judge of the living and the dead."

Have Extraterrestrials Visited Earth in the Past?

In 1956, Morris K. Jessup published a book with the provocative title, *UFOs and the Bible*. In this book, Jessup explained some visions and miracles in the Bible in terms of space aliens interacting with humans. Neither this book, nor the 1963 publication of Virginia F. Brasington's *Flying Saucers in the Bible* attracted much attention. While Jessup attempted to undermine the authority of Scripture, Brasington apparently was a Christian who accepted the idea that in the Bible God often manifested Himself in the form of a flying saucer. Other than this oddity, Brasington appeared to be otherwise orthodox in her beliefs. Perhaps Brasington wrote her book in response to the work of Jessup and others at the time. At any rate, these works did not seem to have much of an impact.

Things dramatically changed in 1968 with the publication of the book, *Chariots of the Gods?* by Swiss author Erich von Däniken (b. 1935). In this book, von Däniken argued that extraterrestrial aliens have visited Earth frequently in the past and thus influenced the development of humanity throughout history. *Chariots of the Gods?* was an instant best-seller, and it established von Däniken as an expert on what has become known as the ancient astronaut hypothesis. Von

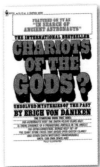

According to *In Search of Ancient Astronauts,* the objects in the top corners of this fresco in the Visoki Dečani Monastery (above the altar) are manned aircraft. But actually, they are medieval representations of the sun and moon, icons often seen in depictions of the Crucifixion during this era of sacred art.

Däniken followed his first book with several others, and the original book was made into a documentary film in 1970. Originally in German, the film was edited and dubbed into English, and it appeared on American television in 1973 as the documentary *In Search of Ancient Astronauts.* Narrated by Rod Serling, the film became quite a sensation in the 1970s. Von Däniken's work inspired many other writers, and so during the 1970s, many more books on the subject appeared.

While interest in the ancient astronaut hypothesis has waned some since the 1970s, its influence is still strong—millions of people today firmly believe in it. In fact, there may be a resurgence of interest in the ancient astronaut hypothesis since the History Channel has run nearly 100 episodes of the *Ancient Aliens* series since the pilot premiered in 2009.

What evidence do supporters of the ancient astronaut hypothesis provide for their ideas? They offer several lines of evidence. One line of evidence involves examining many ancient structures around the world. For instance, the Great Pyramid of Cheops dates long ago to some of the earliest Egyptian dynasties. Yet, the Great Pyramid remained the tallest structure in the world until the Middle Ages. The stones of this pyramid are precisely level, accurately oriented, and have only the smallest of gaps between them. Because the Great Pyramid of Cheops and other ancient structures are so impressive, supporters of the ancient astronaut hypothesis ask the question, "How could ancient man have built these things given the crude technology that they had?"

Created creative

Of course, many readers may already know one possible answer—early man was not as primitive as many people think. If the evolutionary worldview were true, then people gradually evolved from ape-like ancestors. But even after humans took modern form, it took a long time for society and culture to slowly develop. Hence, in the evolutionary view, it took many years for civilization to arise and develop sufficiently in order to build great works, such as the Great Pyramids of Egypt.

But what if creation as described in the Bible is true? Genesis 4:16–17 records that Cain built a city—only one generation removed from Adam. So, according to the biblical worldview, it did not take a long time to develop civilization as in the evolutionary worldview. Furthermore, Genesis 4:18–22 records that within seven generations from Adam men had developed animal husbandry, music, and metal working, again suggesting rapid and early sophistication. Given the vast overlapping lifespans of early man recorded in the Bible that continued for some time after the Flood (Genesis 5:1–32, 11:10–32), there may have been considerable technological progress early in history.

It is quite plausible, then, that early man was very capable of building impressive structures, particularly when lifetimes were still much longer than today's. Indeed, as previously mentioned, the Great Pyramid of Cheops was built very early in Egyptian history, and of the remaining pyramids, the most impressive ones were built early as well. This is a common trend from around the ancient world—many of the most impressive structures date from the earliest epochs. This is the reverse of what one might expect if evolution were true, but exactly what one would expect from the biblical point of view.

Astronauts and statues

Supporters of the ancient astronaut hypothesis, however, generally are committed to evolutionary thinking. They claim that we do not know how ancient structures were built, so they conclude that ancient people must have had alien assistance. However, there are many modern theories of how ancient people built these structures using ramps, levers, ropes, pulleys, and rollers. There have been numerous attempts to demonstrate these theories by replicating ancient building techniques. Many of these projects have been successful; that is, satisfactory replicas of ancient structures were constructed, albeit on a much smaller scale.

Colossi of Memnon.

Photo by Jerzy Strzelecki

Some of the giant moai on Easter Island

While it may be economically feasible to hire a crew of a few dozen men to work for a few days to produce small pyramids, what was the incentive to commit the vast resources required to compel the large work crews over many years for the construction of the largest Egyptian pyramids? We do not know the answer to that question. However, this is not a question of technology, but one of organization of a culture and society.

To illustrate the thinking of those who support the ancient astronaut hypothesis, consider the moai, the famous stone statues of Easter Island. When European explorers arrived in 1722, they found a sparsely populated, treeless island. Because the Polynesian people on Easter Island were considered "primitive," they hardly seemed capable of building and transporting these enormous statues to their current locations. Hence, the origin of the statues remained a mystery. And this fabled mystery was easily translated into a story of ancient astronauts either constructing the statues or guiding the natives of the island in the moai construction. However, this overlooks the possibility that their ancestors were capable of such things.

Consider a far less fantastic explanation. Easter Island is one of the remotest inhabited islands on Earth. Consequently, it was settled late—possibly as late as the early second millennium AD. While the island has been treeless for some time, there is abundant evidence from pollen in the soil that the island was heavily forested a few centuries ago, prior to, and for a few centuries after colonization by the Polynesians. For a while, the abundant wood provided ample fuel and construction materials to support a prosperous and growing society. The islanders probably constructed the moai and then used tools made of wood to move them during this time.

Once the forests on the island were depleted, the society rapidly declined. No longer was wood available to use for fuel, to transport statues, or to build boats for fishing. Without boats, the people of the island likely were stranded. With diminished resources leading to a declining standard of living, the population decreased, and the sophistication of the population retreated. When Westerners found Easter Island, this decline had already happened a few centuries earlier, so the inhabitants of the island appeared incapable of producing the moai—and they were by that time.

Roman remnants

A similar thing happened in much of the Roman world after the collapse of the Roman Empire. The Romans had built large cities supported by superb infrastructure, such as ports, highways, bridges, and aqueducts. Major cities contained elaborate buildings, such as the Colosseum and the Pantheon in Rome. In the chaos that ensued after the collapse of the Roman Empire in the West, the population of major cities declined precipitously. The infrastructure was no longer maintained, and in many cases, was not even used. For many years, travelers to Rome marveled at the vast tracts of abandoned homes and other buildings and the grandeur of structures no longer in use. Eventually, people probably wondered who built these marvelous things and how they had built them. Certainly, a visitor from outside would have realized that the locals in their current state were incapable of such things.

However, since no one at the time could conceive of visitors from other planets, it is unlikely that anyone suggested the ancient astronaut hypothesis.

Landing strips?

Another line of evidence that supporters of the ancient astronaut hypothesis use is various patterns, produced by ancient people, allegedly visible only from the air. The most famous example of this is the Nazca lines, a series of lines in various shapes in southern Peru. Archaeologists believe that the Nazca people produced these lines about fifteen centuries ago. They made the lines by producing shallow trenches through removal of red pebbles on the desert surface exposing the much lighter ground underneath. Many of the lines trace out shapes of various animals and occasionally people. The purpose of the patterns is unknown, but anthropologists and archaeologists have offered various theories, mostly concerning religious observances. Supporters of the ancient astronaut hypothesis claim that these

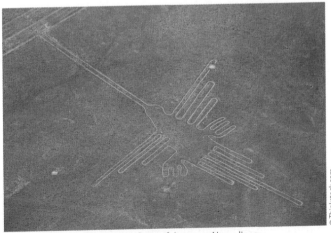

An aerial view of one of the many Nasca lines

patterns can be viewed properly and fully appreciated only from the air. Therefore, they conclude that the Nazca people made these patterns so that aliens flying over the land could see them. Supposedly, the ancient Nazca people thought that the aliens were gods, and so this was an attempt to please those gods. Or perhaps they helped mark landing areas in the same way lights mark runways of airports today.

One key claim of supporters of the ancient astronaut hypothesis is that the patterns in the Nazca lines are visible only from the air. This is not true, however, for many of the patterns are visible from nearby hillsides. While Nazca figures might have been for gods to see, the Nazca people could see them, too. So there is no need to invoke ancient astronauts.

Another proposed evidence for the ancient astronaut hypothesis is the various figures of people from around the world that are

Public Domain

Many believe this ancient statue, which dates to the Jomon era of Japan (1000–400 BC), depicts an alien astronaut

supposedly depictions of alien astronauts. At least one of the Nazca lines patterns is claimed to be this type of depiction. What makes the Nazca man an astronaut? His head is round, and his body is sort of crudely drawn. The claim is that the round head is a helmet, and the crude drawing of the body is a space suit. To many people, the figure looks more like a man drawn by a five-year-old child.

Many Mayan depictions are alleged to be helmeted astronauts operating controls of a space ship. It is the supposed helmets on these human figures that apparently make them astronauts. Almost everyone else recognizes the "helmets" as being head dresses, apparently for some sort of ceremonial purpose. It is unlikely that anyone not predisposed to believe the ancient astronaut hypothesis would view these figures as being space aliens.

Supporters of the ancient astronaut hypothesis also point to similar ancient stone structures scattered worldwide. Most people are familiar with Stonehenge in southern England. Less well known is the fact that there are many similar circular stone structures around the world. Besides being round and constructed of stone, these stone circles have astronomical alignments in common as well. Stones at these sites line up with various rising and setting points of the sun or moon. Most prominent are alignments that coincide with the direction of the rising or setting of the sun on the solstices.

Similarly, pyramids are common in Egypt, Central America, and in many other locations around the world. Supporters of the ancient astronaut hypothesis argue that the best explanation for the similarity of stone circles and pyramids throughout the world is that aliens instructed and perhaps even assisted ancient people in their construction. The alleged purposes of the ancient stone

This well-known pyramid in the ancient city of Teotihuacan
in Mexico is one of the largest in the world

structures vary, but suggestions include navigation aids or communication devices.

More reasonable reasons

Of course, these fanciful suggestions overlook far more plausible explanations. While there is much that we do not know about the purposes of stone circles, certain obvious astronomical alignments are inescapable. They obviously functioned as observatories for marking the passage of time and observing certain dates. This information would be vital in an agricultural society. Related to this may have been ceremonial practices, but we do not know for sure. One ought not to make too much out of their circular shapes because a circle best represents the motions of heavenly bodies. Therefore, the similarity of shape may have been independently discovered numerous times and thus does not constitute evidence of common origin.

Pyramids are trickier. There are claims of astronomical alignments related to pyramids, but those alignments are not nearly as

Public Domain

Stone circles like Stonehenge obviously functioned as observatories for marking the passage of time and observing certain dates

clear as with stone circles. Most Egyptian pyramids functioned as tombs, which appears to have been their primary function. Some Central American pyramids are of much more recent origin than Egyptian pyramids, so their purpose sometimes is easier to trace via historical accounts.

For instance, the Aztecs practiced human sacrifice on many of their pyramids. This coincides with the presence of temples at the summits of many Central American pyramids, which makes them more similar to ziggurats of Mesopotamia than to the pyramids of Egypt. Many people think that ziggurats were inspired by the tower of Babel. If so, it is possible that the construction of pyramids around the world was similarly inspired. As people dispersed throughout the world after the confusion of languages at Babel, they carried and passed on their memory of the great Tower of Babel. Perhaps building pyramids worldwide began as an attempt to reconstruct their lost past.

Alien origins

Many supporters of the ancient astronaut hypothesis go even further, suggesting that extraterrestrials guided evolution of life here on Earth. One proposal is that aliens introduced life on Earth billions of years ago. This is a variation on the idea of panspermia, which is the belief that life did not originate on Earth, but rather that life originated elsewhere and found itself planted on Earth. Normally, panspermia posits that the first living organisms came to Earth accidentally as hitchhikers on rocks ejected off the surface of some other planet on which life existed.

However, the ancient astronaut hypothesis version of panspermia has an ancient civilization either intentionally or unintentionally seeding life on the early Earth. If it was an intentional act, this is known as directed panspermia. In this view it is suggested that the aliens come back to check on us for various reasons from time to time. This idea has been the subject of many science fiction films and novels. Another variation is that extraterrestrial aliens genetically modified ape-like creatures to produce mankind as a much more advanced organism on Earth.

Aliens in the Bible

What supporters of the ancient astronaut hypothesis say about the Bible ought to be of grave concern to Christians. First, let's suppose for the moment that extraterrestrials have used spacecraft to visit Earth. How would these aliens be perceived? We tend to interpret things that we experience in terms of what we know or what we think we know. It is no accident that 1947 ushered in the era of UFO phenomena.

This was just one decade prior to the launch of Sputnik, the first artificial satellite. By that time, people generally were aware that space travel was possible and was likely to commence in the near future. Furthermore, for at least a couple of centuries, people had thought that life existing elsewhere in the universe was possible. Hence, it was relatively easy for many people to interpret things that they saw in terms of extraterrestrial visitations. But how might an alien visitation have been interpreted much earlier?

As we saw in an earlier chapter ("Why All the Interest in UFOs?"), extraterrestrial life is not possible in a geocentric worldview. Since nearly everyone was a geocentrist until just a few centuries ago, the concept of spaceships from other planets was not even conceivable until very recently. How would ancient people have viewed extraterrestrial aliens? Supporters of the ancient astronaut hypothesis conclude that ancient people would have regarded extraterrestrial visitors as gods because of their ability to fly and the wonders of their advanced technologies.

Beginning with this assumption, supporters of the ancient astronaut hypothesis believe that all of the major religions of the world were likely inspired by alien visitations. They teach that many prophets, including the true prophets described in Scripture, had encounters with extraterrestrials. For instance, Moses' encounters with God at the burning bush and on Mt. Sinai supposedly were meetings with extraterrestrials. Von Däniken suggested that the Ark of the Covenant was an electrically charged radio transmitter. In his mind, the transmitter was used to communicate with aliens in spacecraft, and the electrical charge ostensibly explains the death of Uzzah when he touched the ark (2 Samuel 6:6–7).

Furthermore, supporters of the ancient astronaut hypothesis teach that the fiery chariot that took Elijah to heaven (2 Kings 2:11) was a flying saucer. And Ezekiel's first vision (Ezekiel 1:1–28) supposedly was a flying saucer, too. But it doesn't stop there! Supporters of the ancient astronaut hypothesis not only dismiss visions and the audible voice of God as coming from aliens, but they even explain miracles as the actions of aliens. The healings

Public Domain

Matthäus Merian's engraving of Ezekiel's vision (1670)

and raisings from the dead that Jesus and His disciples performed are ascribed to the actions of extraterrestrials. If this explanation is true, then none of the remarkable things recorded in the Bible were accomplished as they were described. Rather, the miracles found in the Bible were no more than alien intervention, not the power of God.

In 1969, a year after von Däniken published his first book, Robert Dione (1922–1996) published *God Drives a Flying Saucer*. Dione went much further than von Däniken in challenging the Bible. Dione taught that God was not simply an alien mistaken for a god by ancient people, but rather an alien that purposely passed himself off as God. Supposedly, another alien, Gabriel, hypnotized and then artificially inseminated Mary  with God's sperm so that she could give birth to Jesus. Dione further taught that our brains are like radios in that they could receive and transmit messages via electromagnetic waves. In this manner, God supposedly can influence people to do things. One of Dione's examples of this is Hitler being instigated to make war against the Soviet Union for its atheism. It remains a mystery whether this alien posing as God caused the Holocaust, or whether this alien could have prevented it. This mind control also explained many of Jesus' miracles, in Dione's estimation. The people that Jesus healed had been impaired by the alien via the manipulation of their brains, and Jesus merely reversed their states.

It is clear that the alien astronaut hypothesis is nothing more than a direct attack upon the accuracy and authority of Scripture. Sadly, there are millions of people in the world today who sincerely believe this rotten explanation of the Bible. In this sense, the entire UFO phenomenon can be viewed as a satanic conspiracy in that people have been deceived, exchanging the truth of God for a lie. What's worse is that all the while that they are deceived, they firmly believe that they are the only ones who see things clearly, which illustrates the futility of man's thinking apart from God (Ephesians 4:17–18). This indeed may be the sort of delusion leading to believing a lie that the Apostle Paul warned about in 2 Thessalonians 2:11–12.

Raëlism: a UFO cult

Von Däniken's alien astronaut hypothesis has spawned at least one cult. The French sports car journalist Claude Vorihon (b. 1946) claimed to have had an encounter with a flying saucer over several days in 1973. According to Vorihon, the spacecraft was flown by the Elohim, an alien race. *Elohim* is a Hebrew title for God, which first appears in Genesis 1:1. In Hebrew, a plural noun is indicated by an *im* ending, so Elohim is plural. The plural form of Elohim is one of

Claude Vorihon, also known as the prophet Raël, founder of the Raëlism UFO cult

majesty. Many Christians also see in the plural form of Elohim a hint of the Trinity in the very first verse of the Bible. Apparently, the plural nature of Elohim gave Vorihon the idea to call the alien race that is supposedly responsible for humanity's existence the Elohim. Vorihon calls an individual member of this supposed alien race an *Eloha*. (Note that the singular form ought to be written in English as *Elohah*.)

One of the Eloha that Vorihon claimed to have met was named Yahweh. *Yahweh* in the Hebrew Bible is the personal name of God. Obviously, Vorihon's use of the Hebrew words *Yahweh* and *Elohim* is an attempt to diminish the authority of Scripture. It also is an attempt to explain away the Bible. By this use, Vorihon was not-so-subtly suggesting that Moses previously had a encounters with Yahweh and the other Elohim.

Yahweh supposedly told Vorihon to establish a new religion. The name of the new religion was to be MADECH, which is an acronym of the French phrase "*m*ouvement pour l'*a*ccueil *d*es *E*lohim *c*réateurs de l'*h*umanité." In English that would be, "movement for welcoming the Elohim, creators of humanity." The purpose of this new religion was to reunite humanity with our creators, the Elohim. The problem was that mankind was too fragmented and warlike. According to Vorihon, the Elohim were desirous of reestablishing a relationship with humanity and taking us to a new level. But many things would need to change in the world before that could happen. People would have to realize their true origin and establish a single, world government to bring about peace and caring for one another. Only then would reunification with our Elohim creators be possible.

Vorihon organized MADECH right away. And in the following year of 1974, more than 2,000 people attended the first MADECH conference. By 1975 changes were already being made. The movement had attracted many UFO enthusiasts, along with many occultists. Vorihon disapproved of the direction that MADECH was taking, such as declining interest in the Elohim as the creator of mankind, so he removed many leaders in the group. A few months later, Vorihon claimed to have spent three days with the Elohim, visiting several places aboard their spacecraft. Vorihon said that he experienced many things during this time, such as meeting great, religious leaders of the past, including Buddha, Jesus, and Mohammed.

Eventually, Vorihon changed his name to Raël, which supposedly means "messenger of the Elohim." Accordingly, MADECH is now known as Raëlism, meaning followers of Raël in parallel to Buddhism and Christianity referring to followers of Buddha or Jesus Christ. Raëlism has now spread around the world with chapters in many countries.

The beliefs of Raëlism are a mix of the alien astronaut hypothesis, technology, peace, and modern ideas of personal freedom. As previously mentioned, Raëlism teaches that the Elohim created man—but this was after they terraformed Earth to make it suitable. Apparently, this terraforming encompassed much of the Genesis creation account. Humanity has now reached a point, technologically speaking, that we can join our creators in doing the same elsewhere. However, we must first achieve a certain level of peace and maturity. Raëlism is atheistic and denies that we are spiritual beings. Rather, the Elohim have recorded our DNA and our memories and have stored them on computers. People who are worthy—based upon their goodness and accomplishments—will be resurrected in the sense that their DNA and memories will be recreated. Presumably, the advanced technology of the Elohim will keep recreated people alive indefinitely, imparting a form of immortality.

As with other purveyors of the alien astronaut hypothesis, the Raëlians teach that the Elohim have intervened at various times to impart important knowledge to humanity. Many biblical prophets are explained by encounters with the Elohim. Obviously, the name Elohim found in the Genesis creation account and the creation account itself supposedly are expressions of information shared with Moses. Other founders of religions, such as Buddha, Mohammed, and even Joseph Smith, are claimed to have been visited by the Elohim.

To aid in advancing humanity, Raël founded the human cloning company Clonaid. In 2002, Clonaid claimed the birth of the first cloned human. They gave the name Eve to this baby. This announcement was met with tremendous skepticism, and many experts view this as a hoax.

Raëlian teaching also has an emphasis on sex. They believe that any sexual activity between consenting adults it good. Hence, Raëlians support homosexuality, bisexuality, pansexuality, and homosexual marriage. In some parts of the world, Raëlians have supported the right of women to go topless in public much as men can do.

Raëlism shares a common theme with other false religions. Mohammed claimed Jesus as an earlier prophet, a prophet second in authority only to Mohammed himself. However, Mohammed taught that Jesus' teachings were misunderstood and perverted, so Mohammed set out to correct those teachings. In a similar manner, Joseph Smith claimed that Jesus' teachings were not properly conveyed, so Smith taught that he was reintroducing proper teaching when he established the Church of Jesus Christ of Latter Day Saints (the Mormons). False religions of more recent origin tend to be more universal in origin—instead of claiming only biblical prophets as their predecessors, many modern false religions include other religions, such as Buddhism, in their lineage. An example of this is Baháʾí, which teaches that there is a unity of religion. By this unity of religion, Baháʾí means that there is one religion that God has progressively revealed through many prophets in various religions and that Baháʾuʾlláh, the founder of Baháʾí, is just the latest prophet. The differences between the universalism of Raëlism and Baháʾí are that in Raëlism there is no God and that the supposed message from the aliens is presumed to be the last one.

Heaven's Gate: a small, tragic cult

Marshall Applewhite (1931–1997), along with Bonnie Nettles (1927–1985), founded the Heaven's Gate cult in the early 1970s. What they created was an odd mix of New Age, UFOs, and science fiction. Using the ancient astronaut hypothesis, Applewhite taught that aliens planted the seeds of humans

Applewhite believed that aliens were traveling in a spaceship accompanying Comet Hale-Bopp.

on Earth millions of years ago. Soon these aliens were going to return to Earth to harvest the few humans prepared to take the next step in human evolution. Applewhite called this next step the "Next Level." In order to take this step, people must alleviate themselves of all connection to this world and human-like characteristics, such as family, friends, and possessions. This self-denial also included eschewing sexuality. Consequently, Applewhite and seven other followers were castrated.

In 1997, Applewhite became convinced that the aliens were about to visit Earth to harvest those people prepared for the Next Level. He was certain that the aliens were traveling in a spaceship accompanying Comet Hale-Bopp that year, and that Nettles, who had died a dozen years earlier, was aboard that space ship already.

Marshall Applewhite, founder of the Heaven's Gate
cult, from one of his recruiting videos

Where did Applewhite get this idea? It possibly came from a pho-
tograph of Comet Hale-Bopp taken by an amateur astronomer
in 1996. The photo had an odd defect near the comet that some
people thought resembled a flying saucer. This got much public-
ity, including coverage on the popular, overnight, AM radio show,
Coast to Coast, hosted by Art Bell.

In order to be picked up by the aliens aboard the spaceship and make it to the Next Level, the members of this cult
had to make the final severance from their humanity—by sui-
cide. Therefore, in March of 1997, 39 members of the Heaven's
Gate cult, including Applewhite, killed themselves. Since this
was most of the membership of Heaven's Gate, this effectively
ended the cult.

These two tragic cults illustrate the danger that the interest in UFOs presents. As I have already shown, belief in ETs is
based upon the assumption of biological evolution. If evolution

is true, then there is no need for God. According to Romans 1:18–32, the rejection of the true and living God leads to all sorts of problems. People's imaginations become vain, and their foolish hearts are darkened. All the while that they profess their wisdom, they become fools. In both the Raëlians and the Heaven's Gate cult, they worship aliens rather than the Creator. With their debauched view of sexuality, the Raëlians certainly are given over to unnatural affections that are spoken of in Romans 1, whereas the Heaven's Gate cult wrongly eschewed sexuality of any kind and ended up taking their own lives. These ends clearly are not what God intends for people. This further reinforces the concept that there is a spiritual component to the widespread interest in UFOs.

What Are We to Think?

So what is a Christian to think about UFOs and ETs? First, we must realize that nearly all discussion about such matters has been within an evolutionary worldview. That worldview assumes the plurality of worlds—that life has arisen on many other planets in the universe, and that life on at least some of those planets is intelligent. Hence, in the evolutionary worldview one might expect that extraterrestrial aliens will visit Earth from time to time.

However, Christians ought not to adopt an evolutionary worldview. Instead, we ought to base what we think upon the Bible, not the ideas of men. Evolution is clearly contrary to Scripture, and so life only exists where God created it. While the Bible does not explicitly state that God created life only on Earth, the clear implication from Scripture is that God made life only on Earth and that man is the center of God's attention. Therefore, within a biblical worldview, one would reject the plurality of worlds idea and would not expect extraterrestrial aliens to have visited Earth (or even to exist).

There is a stark contrast between the biblical and secular worldviews with regard to expectation of extraterrestrials visiting Earth. We have seen in this Pocket Guide that most UFO sightings can be explained in terms of misidentifications or hoaxes. The remaining unexplained sightings cannot be definitively identified as flying saucers. Interestingly, even most scientists who believe in evolution agree with this assessment. Even those scientists who think that the universe is teeming with life generally do not think that the evidence for flying saucers has yet been established. It is often said that "extraordinary claims demand extraordinary evidence." Despite all the books written on flying saucers, there is no clear evidence that a single flying saucer has ever visited Earth. So, the evidence thus far has confirmed the expectation from the biblical worldview.

If there is no clear evidence of alien visitation to Earth, then what are we to make of all the interest in the subject? This brings up a second important point—that there is a spiritual component to the interest in UFOs. In an earlier chapter ("Is There an Alien Invasion of a Different Type?"), we discussed one theory popular with some Christians that UFO phenomena in recent years have been demonic influences as a prelude to end-time events. And in the previous chapter, we saw that the alien astronaut hypothesis provides a direct attack upon the authority of Scripture, suggesting that the miracles of the Bible simply are activities of extraterrestrial aliens.

However, there is a much broader spiritual threat that interest in extraterrestrials presents. Belief in intelligent life on other planets is predicated upon the assumption of the naturalistic origin of life. If life arose on Earth and other planets through natural means, then there is no need of a Creator. If there is no Creator, then there is no such thing as sin. If sin does not exist, then man is not in need of redemption. If there is no need for man's redemption, then the ministry of Jesus Christ as recorded in the New Testament is false. In short, belief in extraterrestrial intelligence is incompatible with Christianity.

It is no accident that people who enthusiastically embrace the belief that extraterrestrials have visited Earth usually have an improper view of the Bible. They either are skeptical toward the Bible, treating it as just a collection of superstitions and stories, or they take a New Age approach and very ecumenically combine Christianity with other religions. Salvation through the atoning work of Jesus Christ is not possible on these terms. Many people remain content in viewing the Bible as less than the authoritative Word of God, effectively hardening their hearts. Since belief in flying saucers from other planets is so effective in condemning so many souls, the entire UFO culture amounts to a satanic deception that points away from Jesus Christ. There is no need for any real visits to this planet by aliens or even manifestations of demonic activity to sustain this culture. All that is required to keep the UFO culture thriving is a continued belief promoted by books, TV specials, popular culture, and now, the internet.

Contrast this to the message of the Bible. God created man without sin. But the first man, Adam, chose to disobey God and thus brought sin and death as the consequence of sin into the world (Genesis 3). To provide for man's redemption, God sent his only begotten Son, Jesus Christ, to atone for our sins (John 3:16). Jesus died for our sins, was buried, but rose from the dead (1 Corinthians 15:3–4). As the disobedience of the first Adam brought sin and death into the world, only the obedience of this last Adam (Jesus Christ) could bring salvation and life (Romans 5:14–19; 1 Corinthians 15:21–22, 15:45–47). All that is required is that we repent of our sin and believe in the sufficiency of this atoning work of Jesus by faith (Acts 16:31, 20:21; Romans 10:9).

Like any other fiction, stories involving ETs can be vehicles to explore all sorts of questions in a literary or artistic manner. And ETs can be fun to fantasize about. However, we must keep in mind that ETs are make-believe, and we must be careful that our make-believe ideas remain in the realm of fiction. For their entertainment and thought-provoking value, I will continue to watch movies and TV shows that may have ETs in them. But I suggest caution to those people who may be tempted to give too much credence to the possibility of ETs and hence undermine a biblical worldview.

Author Biography

Dr. Danny R. Faulkner earned graduate degrees in physics and astronomy and taught at the University of South Carolina Lancaster for over 26 years. Dr. Faulkner is a member of the Creation Research Society and also serves as the editor of the *Creation Research Society Quarterly*. He has written more than a hundred papers in various astronomy and astrophysics journals and is author of *Universe by Design* and *The New Astronomy Book*.

In January 2013, Dr. Faulkner became the full-time astronomer at Answers in Genesis and the Creation Museum. His duties include writing and speaking for Answers in Genesis, overseeing Johnson Observatory, and writing planetarium shows for Stargazers Planetarium.